D0261764

Everyday Eclipses

Roger McGough

Everyday Eclipses

VIKING
an imprint of
PENGUIN BOOKS

086911397

VIKING

Published by the Penguin Group
Penguin Books Ltd, 80 Strand, London WC2R 0RL, England
Penguin Putnam Inc., 375 Hudson Street, New York, New York 10014, USA
Penguin Books Australia Ltd, 250 Camberwell Road, Camberwell, Victoria 3124, Australia
Penguin Books Canada Ltd, 10 Alcorn Avenue, Toronto, Ontario, Canada M4V 3B2
Penguin Books India (P) Ltd, 11 Community Centre, Panchsheel Park, New Delhi – 110 017, India
Penguin Books (NZ) Ltd, Cnr Rosedale and Airborne Roads, Albany, Auckland, New Zealand
Penguin Books (South Africa) (Pty) Ltd, 24 Sturdee Avenue, Rosebank 2196, South Africa

Penguin Books Ltd, Registered Offices: 80 Strand, London WC2R 0RL, England

www.penguin.com

First published 2002
1

Copyright © Roger McGough, 2002

The moral right of the author has been asserted

Set in 11.75/14.5 pt Monotype Bembo
Typeset by Rowland Phototypesetting Limited, Bury St Edmunds, Suffolk
Printed in Great Britain by Clays Ltd, St Ives plc

A CIP catalogue record for this book is available from the British Library

ISBN 0–670–91262–x

For the City of Liverpool

Contents

Everyday Eclipses

The hamburger flipped across the face of the bun
The frisbee winning the race against its own shadow
The cricket ball dropping for six in front of the church clock
On a golden plate, a host of communion wafers
The brown contact lens sliding across the blue iris
The palming of small change
Everyday eclipses.

Out of the frying pan, the tossed pancake orbits
    the Chinese lampshade
The water bucket echoing into the well
The black, snookering the cue ball against the green baize
The winning putt on the eighteenth
The tiddlywink twinking toward the tiddlycup
Everyday eclipses.

Neck and neck in the hot-air balloon race
Holding up her sign, the lollipop lady blots out
    the Belisha beacon
The foaming tankard thumped onto the beermat
The plug into the plughole
In the fruit bowl, the orange rolls in front of the peach
Every day eclipses another day.

Goodbye bald patch, Hello yarmulke
A sombrero tossed into the bullring
Leading the parade, the big bass drum, we hear cymbals
    but cannot see them
One eclipse eclipses another eclipse.

To the cold, white face, the oxygen mask
But too late
One death eclipses another death.

The baby's head, the mother's breast
The open O of the mouth seeking the warm O of the nipple
One birth eclipses another birth
Everyday eclipses.

Greek Tragedy

Approaching midnight and the mezze unfinished
we linger over Greek coffee and consider
calling for the bill, when suddenly the door
bangs open, and out of the neon-starry sky

falls a dazed giant. He stumbles in
and pinballs his way between the tables
nicking ringlets of deep-fried calamari en route.
Nikos appears from the kitchen, nervous but soothing.

'Double moussaka,' grunts the giant,
'and two bottles of that retsina muck.'
He gazes around the taverna, now freeze-framed.
No tables are empty, but none are full.

You could have broken bits off the silence
and dipped them into your taramasalata.
Then he sees me. I turn to a rubberplant
in the far corner and try to catch its eye,

'Excuse me, can I have the bill, please?'
He staggers over and sits down. The chair groans
and the table shudders. 'I know you, don't I?'
he says. '"Lily the Pink" an' all that crap.

'Give us yer autograph. It's not for me,
it's for me nephew. Stick it on this.'
I sign the crumpled napkin as if it were
the Magna Carta and hand it back.

Then to my girlfriend I say overcheerfully,
'Time we were off, love.' While peering
at the napkin as if I'd blown my nose into it
he threatens: 'Youse are not goin' nowhere.'

On cue, a plate of cheesy mince and two bottles
appear. Flicking our hands from the top of the glasses
he refills them and looks at me hard. Very hard.
'D'ye know who I am?' (I do, but pretend I don't.)

'Eddie Mason. Call me Eddie.' 'Cheers, Eddie.'
'D'ye know what I do?' (I do, but pretend I don't.)
'I'm a villain. Livin' on the edge. Bit like you,
Know what I mean? (I don't, but pretend I do.)

'I'm in the people business like yourself.'
Lest I am a doubting Thomas, he grabs my hand
and shoves a finger into a dent in his skull.
'Pickaxe. And feel tha' . . . and tha' . . . and tha'.'

Brick, hammer, knife, screwdriver, baseball bat.
He takes me on a guided tour of his scalp.
A map of clubs and pubs, doorways and dives.
Of scores settled and wounds not yet healed.

What he couldn't show me were the two holes
above the left eye, where the bullets went in
a fortnight later. Shot dead in the back of a cab
by the father of a guy whose legs he'd smashed

with an iron bar. He hardly touched
his moussaka, but he ordered more wine.
And it goes without saying, that he shredded
the napkin, and left without paying.

The Terrible Outside

The bus I often took as a boy to visit an aunt
went past it. From the top deck I would look
beyond the wall for signs of life: a rooftop protest,
a banner hung from cell windows. I would picture
the escape. Two men sliding down the rope
and legging it up Walton Vale. Maybe hijacking
the bus and holding us hostage. But I'd talk
them round. Share my sweets and pay their fares.

Years later I am invited there to run a poetry
workshop. An escapism easily contained.
And as I check in and pass through security,
and as door after door clangs open and shut,
I imagine that I am a prisoner. 'But I'm innocent,
I tell you. I was framed.' It's no use protesting,
take the old lag's advice, just keep your head down
and get on with it. The three hours will soon pass.

A class of eighteen. All lifers in their early twenties,
most with tatoos, childishly scratched and inked in.
Nervous, I remove my raincoat and shake my
umbrella. 'It's terrible outside,' I say. Then panic.
'I mean, compared to life inside it's not terrible . . .
It's good. It was the weather I was talking about.
Outside, it's really bad. But not as bad as in here,
of course. Being locked up . . . it must be terrible.'

They look at me blankly, wondering perhaps
if that was my first poem and not thinking much of it.
We talk. I read my stuff and they read theirs.
I answer questions (about fashion and music).
The questions I want to ask I can't. 'Hands up
those who killed their fathers? Hands up
those who killed more than once? Hands up . . .'
But those hands are clean, those faces bright.
Any one of them I'd trust with my life.

Or would I? Time's up and the door clangs open.
They all gather round and insist on shaking my hand.
A hand that touches women, that lifts pints, a hand
that counts money, that buttons up brand-new shirts.
A hand that shakes the hand of the Governor,
that raises an umbrella and waves down a cab.
A hand that trembles and clenches and pushes
itself deep into a raincoat pocket. A hand
that is glad to be part of the terrible outside.

'What does your father do?'

At university, how that artful question embarrassed me.
In the common-room, coffee cup balancing on cavalry twills
Some bright spark (usually Sociology) would want an answer.
Shame on me, as feigning lofty disinterest, I would hesitate.

Should I mumble 'docker' in the hope of being misheard?
('There he goes, a doctor's son, and every inch the medical man.')
Or should I pick up the hook and throw it down like a gauntlet?
'Docker. My dad's a docker.' A whistle of corduroy.

How about? 'He's a stevedore, from the Spanish "estibador"
Meaning a packer, or loader, as in ship.' No, sounds too
On the Waterfront, and Dad was no Marlon Brando.
Besides, it's the handle they want not the etymology.

'He's a foreman on the docks.' A hint of status? Possibly.
A touch of class? Hardly. Better go with the straightforward:
'He works on the docks in Liverpool,' which leaves it open.
Crane-driver? Customs and Excise Officer? Canteen manager?

Clerk? Chairman of the Mersey Docks and Harbour Board?
In bed, I'd hear him naming the docks he knew and loved.
A mantra of gentle reproach: *Gladstone, Hornby, Alexandra,*
Langton, Brocklebank, Canada, Huskisson, Sandon, Wellington,

Bramley Moor, Nelson, Salisbury, Trafalgar, Victoria.

An Apology

Sincere apologies, too late I know, for not getting engaged
on the night we'd planned, Christmas Eve 1962. I had the ring
in my pocket, the one we'd bought together that November
from the little jewellers on Whitefriargate in Hull. Remember?

After Midnight Mass arm-in-arming back to ours,
we linger outside the gates of Seaforth Park. The moon
smiling and expectant. No wind, no people, no cars.
Sheets of ice are nailed to the streets with stars.

The scene is set, two lovers on the silver screen.
A pause, the copy-book kiss. Did angels sing?
This was my moment, the cue to pledge my troth,
to take out the blue, velvet box, and do my stuff.

But marriage was a bridge I feared might be detonated,
And I had this crazy idea that if I didn't mention it, then you
wouldn't either. That we'd collude in romantic amnesia.
That life would go on as before. What could be easier?

Christmas passed. Enraged, you blew up. I felt the blast.
We got engaged. It didn't last.

Bob Dylan and the Blue Angel

What benign stroke of fate took Bob Dylan
to the Blue Angel Club after a gig at the Liverpool Empire
in 1965 remains a mystery. But there he was, seemingly alone,
all tousled up and shy, with Cilla goofing at the bar,
and Freddie Starr on stage downstairs.

Alan 'The man who gave the Beatles away' Williams
introduced us. 'He's a poet too.' So we talked poets and poetry,
music and lyrics, and soon we'd talked our way out of the club,
away from the noise and the crowd
and into the history of rock 'n' roll.

At the intersection of Bold Street and Hardman Street
he stopped. 'I'm at the crossroads, Rog,' he said.
'I can see that, Bob,' I said. 'No, I mean my career,
I don't know which way to turn.' 'Seems clear to me, mate,
let's have a coffee and I'll put you straight.'

So over cappucino in the Picasso I laid it all out.
Dump the acoustic. Forget the folksy stuff and go electric.
Get yourself a band. I remember the look on his face.
Sort of relief. The tension in the trademark
hunched shoulders seemed to melt away.

Hit the booze, make friends with cocaine
to get that druggy feel. Divorce your wife, the pain will pay off
in hard-won lyrics. His eyes closed, the bottom lip trembled.
Poet to poet, you asked for my advice.
I'm not here to give you an easy ride.

Ten years from now you'll be an icon. Sounds nice
but trust me, go against the flow. Dismantle the status.
Reinvent yourself. Embrace the faith of your fathers
then give Christianity a go. With nothing to lose
make albums that serve to confound and confuse.

Then consolidate. A Lifetime Achievement Award,
and then perhaps an Oscar. By the time you're sixty . . .
He smiled, 'Hold on there, boy, we ain't never
gonna grow old.' 'You're right, Bob.' We laughed
and made our way back to his hotel.

On the moonlit steps of the Adelphi
we exchanged phone numbers and addresses.
Suddenly he looked young and vulnerable.
Mumbling his thanks he hurried towards the entrance.
'Don't forget to write,' I called. But he never did. Never did.

Hey, Dude

Paul has probably forgotten about the incident by now
But I clearly remember that Saturday morning
In the sun-filled drawing room of his elegant home
In St Johns Wood. His brother Michael and I
Relaxing over coffee and the morning papers
When he came bounding in like a young puppy.

'I've gorra new song, d'ye wanna hear it?' Needless
To say, we nodded and lowered our newspapers.
He was already at the baby grand. 'It's a gear tune,
But I haven't got the words sorted yet,' he explained
By way of introduction, and then began to sing:
'Hey, dude, get off of my cloud. *Dumpty dumpty*

Di dumpty three is a crowd *di dumpty dum di dumpty*
Dumpty dum Or I'll push you off like Humpty Dumpty.'
And so on and so on. And as the final chord faded
Michael and I made the required appreciative noises.
To have done otherwise would have seemed churlish.
'No, seriously,' he said, 'what do you really think?'

I knew from the way he was looking directly at me
That it was the truth he wanted. 'To be honest, Macca . . .'
I hesitated, but his eyes were begging me to continue.
'I think that the lyrics are working against the melody.
There's a lovesong in there, trying to get out, but . . .
Well, it sounds more like Jagger than McCartney.'

The reference to the Stones brought him to his feet.
To underline my point Michael sang the opening bars
Of 'Get off of my cloud' while his brother, head lowered,
Leaned against the piano as if his world might collapse.
I had to think on my feet, so I stood up and said,
'What about "Hey, Jude?" You know, use a girl's name?'

Paul looked puzzled. 'That's a funny name for a bird.'
'It's short for Judith,' I explained with all the confidence
Of someone having it off with a girl called Judith.
'Forget the dude. Forget pushing people off clouds.
Forget Humpty Dumpty. Think of the lovely Jude
And you've got another number one on your hands.'

He didn't say anything before going back upstairs
But the gentle squeeze of my shoulder spoke volumes.
And as we left the house we could hear his guitar
As he unpacked his rich mind-hoard of love lyrics.
Outside, Michael and I selected a couple of the likeliest-
looking Beatles groupies and whizzed them down to the pub.

A Bolt from the Blue

In no way am I trying to lay claim
to kickstarting the career of Jimi Hendrix.
What took place that night might well have
happened anyway. But please hear me out.

The early sixties. At the Scotch of St James
in the heart of Mayfair, a meagre crowd
has turned up to witness Jimi's first UK
appearance. It was an embarrassment.

After the show, Chas Chandler came over
to ask if, as one of the only real celebrities there,
I would pop backstage to offer a few words
of advice and comfort to the young man.

Smaller in real life, he was languishing
on a velvet settee looking for all the world
like a black Little Lord Fauntleroy.
He groaned: 'I ain't never gonna play again.'

As I was about to protest, he picked up a cloth
and began to wipe the neck of his banjo.
It was then that I had the idea.
It came to me like a bolt from the blue.

Thank U Very Much

Taking a break from recording at Olympic Studios
the Gallaghers, large as life, were outside my local
that August evening, when, pen and notebook in hand
I strolled past as inconspicuously as possible.

But in vain. It was Noel who recognized me
and well-nigh dragged me over to their table.
Liam bought the round: red wine for his brother,
large whiskey for himself, and a lager top for me.

'Tell us about John Lennon.' 'Tell us about the Sixties.'
'Tell us about . . .' A double-act that was difficult
to penetrate. 'Relax, lads,' I said, 'well understand
your excitement, but one at a time, please.'

'Tell us about Scaffold.' 'Tell us about Brian Epstein.'
'Calm down, calm down,' I said with Aintree irony.
'If you're really interested, why not hit my web-site?'
Liam removed his shades.　　　　　'Gob-shite.'

The One About the Duck

This duck walked into a pub
and went straight up to the bar.
The barman made a joke about
not serving ducks under eighteen
and tried to shoo it out.

But the duck would not be shoon.
It waddled around to the back bar
quacking as it were last orders
to the few remaining customers
in the Sun Inn that afternoon.

So the barman fetched the barmaid
who tried to show the duck the door.
But the duck would not be shown.
So the barman fetched the manager,
but the three of them had no luck.

Seeking guidance from above, the manager
brought down the landlord and his wife,
and all five, armed with tea towels,
cornered the duck between the Ladies
and the fruit machine and overpowered it.

They were gentle, they were kind,
and their concern was for the welfare
of the web-footed intruder, the green-headed
alien away from his loved ones
and longing for home, Quack Quack.

So the landlord, followed by the landlady,
the manager, the barman and the barmaid
carried the duck, swaddled in tea towels,
across the High Street to the pond
that lies in the middle of the green.

'There you go, Donald, you naughty duck,'
said the landlord setting it free.
And his staff were pleased with their good deed,
and so, totally unprepared for the commotion
that followed. The sudden violence and murder.

Angels at four o'clock. While two fastened
on to its bill keeping it closed, the others
pecked and stabbed, turned it over
and dragged it under. Helpless, the rescuers
watched it drown in a bullseye of bubbles.

Stunned, they returned to the Sun
and tried to make sense of it all.
Synchronized drowning, bloodlust or justice?
Heads down, tails up, dabbling free.
Have you heard the one about the duck? No joke.

Honey and Lemon

Jogging around Barnes Common one April morning
when a rat crossed my path twenty metres ahead.
A fat, furry fist spelling danger from the tip
of its pointed nose to the end of its pointing tail.

Dogs daily, magpies frequently, rats? Never.
So, curious, I swerved left into the undergrowth
and took the overgrown path back to where
the beast (it had doubled in size) had scuttled.

Three strides along and there it was, barring
my way like a rival gang of football hooligans.
Red-eyed and snuffling, PLAGUE written all over it.
Motionless, I tried to stifle the fear rising within.

Having read in one of those survival handbooks
that rats love lemon, I spat the honey and lemon
pastille I was sucking straight into the bushes,
and sure enough, the brute dived in after it.

Unfortunately for the rat, a huge grizzly bear,
mad for honey, came crashing through the trees
and tore the creature to pieces with its iron claws.
By then, I was back on the road sprinting for home.

Bees Cannot Fly

Bees cannot fly, scientists have proved it.
It is all to do with wingspan and body weight.
Aerodynamically, they are incapable of sustained flight.
Bees simply cannot fly. And yet they do.

There's one there, unaware of its dodgy ratios,
A noisy bubble, a helium-filled steamroller.
Fat and proud of it, buzzing around the garden
As if it were the last day of the spring sales.

Trying on all the brightest flowers, squeezing itself
Into frilly numbers three sizes too small.
Bees can fly, there's no need to prove it. And sting.
When stung, do scientists refuse to believe it?

My Life in the Garden

It is a lovely morning, what with the sun, etc.
And I won't hear a word said against it.

Standing in the garden I have no idea of the time
Even though I am wearing the sundial hat you gave me.

What the scene requires is an aural dimension
And, chuffed to high heaven, birds provide it.

I think about my life in the garden
About what has gone before

And about what is yet to come.
And were my feet not set in concrete,

I would surely jump for joy.

Flight Path

A nice day for breakfast outside. Well-practised,
by now, birds sing out the end of summer.
On the wall, a marmalade sphinx, unblinking
doesn't miss a twitch in the garden.

In a hurry for Heathrow and bored,
a 747 scratches its dirty fingernails
down the clearblue, blameless sky.
We wince, the birds, the cat and I.

★

Across the pond, excited at the prospect ahead
they are up at first light and praying. The drive
out to Logan will be uneventful. At check-in
a girl will thank them and smile: 'Have a nice day.'

Don't Read All About It

He's there everyday on the corner,
the Bad News Vendor. The latest editions
hot off the press, the blood not yet dry.

The headlines scream again of murder.
A six-year old girl. Part of a city. A small
civilization. In vain, he cries out:

'Don't read all about it! Don't read all about it!'

On the Point of Extinction

Manx: The celtic dialect (Manx Gaelic) of the Isle
of Man, now on the point of extinction.

Pears Encyclopaedia, 78th edition

An old man walks into his local newsagents
and asks, in perfect Manx, for a packet of Silk Cut
and the *Daily Mirror* . . . Oh, and some aspirin
for the missus. The man behind the counter,
being new to the area, says, 'Pardon?'

Tobaccoless, paperless and aspirinless,
the old man returns home to find his wife
collapsed on the living-room floor.
He telephones immediately for an ambulance,
but the girl from the Emergency Services Provider,
being in Manchester, says, 'Pardon?'

The old man rushes out into the busy street
and in pure Manx Gaelic appeals for help
to the passers-by. They either nod sympathetically
and give directions to the ferry, or say, 'Pardon?'

The old woman dies. The old man is struck dumb.
And Manx Gaelic, having nobody to talk to,
sets off in search of the Land of Lost Tongues
as fast as his three legs can carry him.

On Having a First Book of Poetry Published
(The day the world ended.)

Oh, what dreadful timing! It couldn't have been worse
For that long-awaited, ground-breaking volume of verse.

A title to die for, an immaculate cover,
Cool photo on the back, then Bang it's all over.

Your publisher hired a publicist to titillate the press
(a review already promised in the TLS, no less).

Fingers crossed for Waterstones and a window display
The launch in Covent Garden, and the following day

a signing at Harrods (you've dreamed of this for yonks)
Practising your signature, you wore out two Mont Blancs.

Then the poetry-reading circuit (50 mins, plus Q & A)
Dropping by at bookstores and libraries on the way.

A choice of Literary Festivals (Cheltenham, Hay-on-Wye)
Chats on local radio, and perhaps one day on Sky.

But, oh, what lousy timing, how could anybody guess
Your career as a poet would last an hour or less.

Yes, it would have been marvellous, it would have been splendid
If you hadn't had it published on the day the world ended.

It's a Jungle Out There

On leaving the house you'd best say a prayer
Take my advice and don't travel by train
As Tarzan said to Jane, 'It's a jungle out there.'

I'm not a man who will easily scare
But I'd rather lick maggots than get on a plane.
On leaving the house you'd best say a prayer.

Skateboards are lethal on top of a stair
A broken back means you'll not walk again
As Tarzan said to Jane, 'It's a jungle out there.'

When the sky turns purple better beware
Bacillus on the breeze and acid in the rain
On leaving the house you'd best say a prayer

Avoid beef like the plague or your plague will be rare
Alcopops slowly eat away the brain
As Tarzan said to Jane, 'It's a jungle out there.'

Don't drink the water and don't breathe the air
For the sake of the children repeat the refrain:
On leaving the house you'd best say a prayer
As Tarzan said to Jane, 'It's a jungle out there.'

Pure Jaguar

Dark clouds. The fresh smell of new rain. The soft hiss
of rubber on smooth, wet bitumen. A reflection in a window:
*a powerful, deep-chested, stocky cat with a large rounded
head and short sturdy limbs.* This is the most technically
well-endowed road-going jaguar yet.

*The fur varies from pale gold to a rich, rust red,
and is patterned with a series of dark rosettes
that enclose one or two smaller spots.* The body
isn't just stunningly handsome, it's also 30% stiffer
on twist than the previous class leader.

*Being good climbers, jaguars often rest in trees,
but are believed to hunt almost entirely on the ground.*
That makes it a superb platform from which to mount
an extraordinarily supple, yet at the same time,
tightly controlled suspension package.

Using urine, tree scratches and calls to mark their boundaries
jaguars are not, and never will be commonplace.
A jaguar is special and the X-type is more special still.
*It will feed on almost anything including lizards, snakes,
turtles,* front, side and curtain airbags.

The jaguar's powerful jaws, robust canine teeth,
and the cool integrity of sculptured steel, enable it
to kill livestock weighing 3 or 4 times its own weight,
often with a bite to the back of the skull. The ambience
that is, quite simply, pure jaguar.

This poem is a cut-up of a wildlife conservation leaflet
and a sales brochure for Jaguar Motors.

Learning to Read

Learning to read during the war
wasn't easy, as books were few
and far between. But Mother
made sure I didn't go to sleep
without a bedtime story.

Because of the blackout
the warm, comforting glow
of a bedside lamp was not permitted.
So Mum would pull back the curtains
and open wide the window.

And by the light of a blazing factory
or a crashed Messerschmidt,
cuddled up together, she would read
saucebottles, jamjars, and, my
all-time favourite, a tin of Ovaltine.

So many years ago, but still
I remember her gentle guidance
as I read aloud my first sentence:
'S-p-r-i-n-k-l-e   t-w-o   h-e-a-p-e-d
t-e-a-s-p-o-o-n-s-f-u-l   o-f . . .

In Two Minds

What I love about night
>is the silver certainty of its stars

What I hate about stars
>is the overweening swank of their names

What I love about names
>is that every complete stranger has one

What I hate about one
>is the numerical power it wields over its followers

What I love about followers
>is the unseemly jostle to fill the footsteps

What I hate about footsteps
>is the way they gang up in the darkness

What I love about darkness
>is the soft sighing of its secrets

What I hate about secrets
>is the excitement they pack into their short lives

What I love about lives
>is the variety cut from the same pattern

What I hate about pattern
>is its dull insistence on conformity

What I love about conformity
>is the seed of rebelliousness within

What I hate about within
>is the absence of landscape, the feel of weather

What I love about weather
>is its refusal to stay in at night

What I hate about night
>is the silver certainty of its stars

31

Meeting the Poet at Victoria Station

A day off for you to recover from jetlag
and then the tour begins in Brighton.
Neither met nor talked, but I like your poems
and the face on the back of your Selected.

No sign of you under the station clock
nor at the ticket office, so I make my way
to platform 12. Do I hear castanets?
Tap dancers busking for the pure fun of it?

No. Sitting on the floor, back to the wall
surrounded by bags, books and foolscap,
a woman is pounding a typewriter, oblivious
of commuters stepping around and over her.

You are dressed all in black, wearing glasses,
and your hair is wilder than in the photograph.
Not too late for me to turn back and ring
the Arts Council: 'Laryngitis' . . . 'Gingivitis' . . . 'St Vitus'

Instead, I ask you to dance. You give me your hand
and I whisk you across the marble floor,
my arm around your waist in the old-fashioned way.
Waltz, Foxtrot, Villanelle, Quickstep.

Ticket inspectors clear the way for us
as I guide you in and out of Knickerbox.
Shoppers stop and applaud as we twirl
around the shelves of W.H. Smith and Boots.

A Tango so erotic that Victoria blushes.
Rush hour but nobody is going anywhere
except in a centipedic circle as we lead
the customers in a Conga round the concourse.

A voice over the tannoy: 'Take your partners . . .'
Rumba, Samba, Salsa, Sestina.
Things are hotting up as the tempo quickens
Charleston, Terza Rima, Cha Cha Cha.

Suddenly the music stops.
'Excuse me,' I say, 'are you the poet?'
Removing her glasses she looks up from the typewriter.
'How did you guess?' I help carry her bags to the train.

The Logic of Meteors

August in Devon and all is rain. A soft rain
that seems, not to fall from the sky, but to rise
from the ground and drape itself over the trees
and hedgerows like a swirl of silver taffeta.
But I am not interested in matters meteorological.
Not for me the logic of meteors, but the logic of metre.
For this is a Poetry Course and I am the Tutor.

Last night I had a visitor. (Not a female student:
'I'm having trouble with my sestina' . . . 'Please come in . . .'
But a monster that kamikazied around the room
before ensnaring itself within the vellum lampshade.
Waiting until the moth, light-headed, went into free fall
I clumped it with Ted Hughes' *Birthday Letters*
bringing to an end its short and insubstantial life.

Consumed with guilt? Hardly. A frisson of imagined
Buddhism? Possibly. Would Mrs Moth and the kids
be at home waiting? Unlikely. It was either me or it.
For who is to say that my visitor wasn't a mutant killer
waiting for me to fall asleep before stuffing itself
down my throat and bringing to a suffocating end
this short and insubstantial life . . . Do I hear thunder?

★   ★   ★

A second meteor, a host-carrier bearing aliens from
the Planet of the Moths, tears a hole in the damp taffeta
at the hem of the hills surrounding Black Torrington.
A soft rain still, but high above, a vellum moon.
In his room, the Tutor pours himself a large scotch,
guiltily wipes the smear of blood from the dust-jacket
and settles down, unaware of the avenging, impending swarm.

Toffee

It gives me no pleasure to say this
But he won't be missed.
Resentful when sober, aggressive when pissed.

Though not proven, it is rumoured
That he pays to be spanked.
And worse, he can't write for toffee.

Small magazine stuff over the years.
The same poem thinly disguised.
Recycled, retitled, endlessly revised.

I would like to say that book launches
Will never be the same
Without his snide comments.

That literary gatherings will seem tame
Without his drunken outbursts.
But I can't.

It does me no credit to say this
But in his sad case,
Posthumous the better.

Memento Mori

I still have the blue beret that JFK
was wearing the day he was assassinated.

If you take the nipple between finger and thumb,
hold it up to the light and twirl it round

you can see the bullet holes (or, to be precise,
the two holes made by a single bullet).

For many years I kept in store, the fox-fur stole
that Virginia Woolf wore in March 1941

when she walked into the River Ouse at Rodmell.
But those sharp, little eyes had seen too much.

They disturbed me so I disposed of it.
This leather jacket, however, I would not sell

for a million pounds. Her Royal Highness
was wearing it on that dreadful night in Paris

when her Harley-Davidson skidded on black ice.
This may interest you. John Berryman's silver

fob watch, still showing 9.24. The exact time
he hit the frozen river. Minneapolis, 1972.

Two Riddles

(i)

To ease us
Through those difficult days

At hand to tease out
Waifs and strays

Though causing pain
We squeeze you again

And again. Vain? Not really
More a fear of the unruly

If you wish to borrow mine
Simply repeat the opening line.

(ii)

A rat (black) rattles across the floor
A cross (red) daubed upon the door.

A bell (muffled) rung in the early dawn
A grave (deep) dug far away from town.

A tumbril (full) trundles down the lane
Tomorrow (and tomorrow) it will trundle again.

People avoid me like the plague
What am I?

After the Reading

'Where do you get your ideas from?'
said the lady in fur coat and trainers,
holding out a book for me to sign.

'Do you mind if I sit down, I'm all of a tizzy?
You must excuse me, I haven't been myself
since it happened. Three weeks ago and I'm still shaking.

I was walking down the road minding nobody's
business but my own, when, suddenly,
it leaped out at me. There was no escape.

My back to the railings. Straight out of Hitchcock
it was. A nightmare. I fought to protect myself
from this mad thing that was going for my throat.

Then a man's voice cried out, "Get in. Get in."
He'd pulled up and was holding the car door open.
But before I could close it after me the dog leaped in.

It went for his face. There was blood everywhere.
And the screaming. People on the pavement screaming.
Straight out of Hitchcock it was. Blood and screaming.

That's why I'm like this now, you see. I can't relax.
Three weeks ago and the police haven't done nothing.
More concerned about the dog than me. I rang up.

"It belonged to a farmer," they said, "but it's fine now."
"So bloody what," I said, "but what about me?"
"That's a civil matter," they said, "not criminal."

"Criminal? It's bloody surreal." I was standing there
bandaged up to my elbow, drugged up to the eyeballs,
cradling the telephone like a baby. "What about me?"

"Don't worry," said the policeman, "the dog's fine.
As a matter of fact, he's lying here in front of me
on the lino eating a sheep's head. Happy as Larry."

I couldn't believe my ears. Who's mad? I thought
to myself. Who's mad?' She gave me back the book.
'Would you mind putting the date on as well, please?'

A Fine Tooth Comb

When granny was young she was famous for her teeth.
Although, not so much for her teeth
as for the thick golden hair that covered them.
Unusual, even for those days.

But that blonde smile was her crowning glory
and last thing at night, she would gargle
with shampoo before combing her teeth,
or brushing with a pocket-sized Mason & Pearson.

They were the pride of Halifax, and many a lad
came a-calling, until Ted. Love at first sight
they were married the following year.
Then came the war and the long march into night.

As granny grew older her teeth fell out
one by one, and her hair turned grey.
And today, she has but a single tooth
set in a thin curtain of silver.

Alone now, but the nightly ritual continues
as she takes from her dressing-table drawer
'A present to my one and only girl'
from Ted who went to war and didn't come home.

Polished rosewood inlaid with pearl:
A fine tooth comb.

The Lottery

At five o'clock our time a killer was fried
According to law he was sentenced and died
Georgia the state where they favour the chair
When the switches were thrown I was washing my hair
Just lucky I guess.

At a quarter to midnight on his way to the shop
A stolen car hit him, revved up didn't stop
On arrival at Casualty he was found to be dead
When they rang up his wife I was reading in bed
Just lucky I guess.

At thirteen o nine it went out of control
The port engine failed and it started to roll
Imagine the scene on that ill-fated plane
When it burst into flames I was dodging the rain
Just lucky I guess.

At twenty fifteen it was 9, 24,
11 and 7, only needed three more
As each number came up I hardly could speak
Until I remembered . . . No ticket this week
Unlucky I guess.

Halfway up the mountain it stops. Slips back.
Judders. Slips again. '*Scheisse!*' screams a Fraulein,
'*Scheisse!*' Word for word, you think exactly
the same in English. Two little maids in white dresses,
toting Prada bags, think the same in Japanese.
The wind rocks the cradle, but not gently.

No driver. No door handles on the inside.
Reassuringly there is a hammer for smashing
windows in case of emergency. But is this
an emergency, or just the run up to one?
Unsure of the etiquette, better wait until the carriage
bursts into flames or fills up with water.

'*Scheisse!*' It slides back down the track.
Stops. Slides again. Stops and sways dizzily.
The German girl is on the floor sobbing,
her husband unable to comfort her.
A Texan, the life and soul, makes a joke
about the Big Dipper, but nobody laughs.

A voice crackles over the tannoy. *Pardon?*
If it were writing it would be illegible.
Why are there no Italians on board? Obviously
they've heard the rumours. So what did it say?
'Help is on its way', or, 'Emergency, you fools!
The hammer, use the bloody hammer!'

A power failure. Your lives hang on a thread
(albeit a rusty metal one circa 1888). A winch
turns and the long haul up begins. You hold
your breath. Twenty metres. Stop. Shudder,
and a sickening fall for ten. A tooth being
slowly drawn out and then pushed back in.

Should the cable break the descent will not be
death defying. The view below is breathtaking
but you have no wish to be part of it. Like the
muzzle of a mincing machine, the station waits
to chew you up and spit out the gristly bits
into the silver kidney bowl that is Lake Como.

An hour and a half later the tug-of-war ends
and the passengers alight heavily. The Brits to seek
an explanation. The Americans to seek compensation.
The Germans to seek first aid, and the Japanese,
seemingly unfazed, to seek a little shop that sells
snow-globes and model funicular railway sets.

Tsutsumu

Tsutsumu: The Japanese art of wrapping items in an attractive and appropriate way.

Dear Satoshi,
Thank you for the egg. Smashed in transit, I'm afraid.
The origami chicken that it came in, however,
although gooey was exquisite. How clever you are!

We hesitated for ages before gently dismantling
the Taj Mahal. Perhaps now we regret it.
My wife is over the moon with the curry powder.

It seemed a shame to unpick the delicate spinning-wheel.
Straight out of an enchanted castle, we thought!
The plastic thimble will surely come in handy.

The walnut tree was so lifelike
we considered replanting it in our little garden.
Thank you for the walnut.

And that salmon! The magic you weave with paper!
It seemed to shimmer with life and jump for joy.
Sadly the slice of sashumi was well past its sell-by.

When the life-size model of a Toyota Landcruiser
was delivered, we were as tickled as the postman!
Our thanks for the jasmine-scented car-freshener.

Finally, a note of apology.
It was only after we had broken the string,
torn off the paper, and smashed open the box,
that we realized we had destroyed your gift
of a beautiful box. Sorry.

For one magical moment you imagine
you are at the wheel of a moon-blanch'd
powerboat, speeding across a calm sea
towards the white cliffs of Dover.

But no, you are here on the darkling plain
powerless, as it comes roaring in.
You shout its name into the wind:
'Tsunami, Tsunami', over and over.

Sleep Over

No, I'd rather stand, thank you. Sorry it's so late
but I wanted to get the girls settled down for the night.
Yes, they're sharing Emma's bedroom. Still awake, of course,
I could hear them chattering away as I slipped out.

Yes, I know they shouldn't be left alone in the house
that's why I want to get this business settled quickly.
I've brought over the film script you unwisely rejected.
The one about the producer whose daughter is kidnapped

by a psychopathic screenwriter. All you do is get it made.
You own the company, you're head of production.
Just do it. Naomi is a lovely kid. Hear what I'm sayin'?
Don't worry, I'll see myself out. Goodnight.

Persimmons

Watching the video last night was good.
The four of us stretched out on two sofas
after fish and chips. Lights dimmed.

Soon the heroine, a distracted single mum
with three kids in the red-neck South,
is in deep, deep trouble. Satanism.

Haddock, mushy peas and a large Sprite.
In her nightmare, someone is on the bed
trying to strangle her. She wakes in a sweat.

'*Pause*' to put the kettle on. The youngest
is happy to be put to bed. A story,
but only short because it is Saturday.

'*Play.*' As she hangs out the washing on the line,
her dead mother approaches with a basket of persimmons.
All the scarier for not being a nightmare.

My son is puzzled by the plum-like orange fruit,
and while discussing its taste and origins
we miss the psycho with the baseball bat.

'*Stop.*' '*Rewind?*' No, let her stay for ever
in the deep deep South. Eating forbidden fruit.
Hanging out the nightmares with her dead mother.

Porno Poem

I felt dirty having to write this poem
But an obscene amount of cash was on offer
And had I refused you can be sure
That another poet would have rushed in.
As the reader of course, you are under
No obligation to get involved. Feel free to go.

(Cue music)
A woman with no clothes on is lying on a bed.
A man with no clothes on enters the bedroom.
They do sex. *(Cue FX sighs, groans, etc)*

There. That's the porno done and dusted
And to be honest, I'm glad that it's over.
However, as you chose to read on
Perhaps you now regret having taken part
In the whole sordid affair. Especially
As you were the only one not getting paid.

The Theatre

On arriving at the theatre in good time there was no queue
so I collected my ticket and passed through the empty foyer.
I bought a programme and called in briefly at the bar
before settling into my seat in the centre stalls.

I opened the programme to find that every page was blank
and was on the point of returning to the foyer to complain
when the house-lights began to fade. At that moment
I realized that I was completely alone in the auditorium.

But it didn't matter, because when the curtain rose
and the stage was flooded with light . . . nothing happened.
The only sound was the buzzing of the electrics
The only movement, the occasional ripple of the back-cloth.

Reluctantly at first I watched an empty space
thinking, I am watching an empty space. Then slowly
the emptiness within me began to fill the vacuum without.
Too soon the safety curtain like a dull screen-saver.

To avoid the usual crush I had taken the precaution
of ordering my interval drinks before the performance.
And alone in the bar sipped my whiskey impatiently
until the first bell called me back to my seat.

Though similar in every respect, the second half
was even better than the first, and internalizing,
I could more easily interpret the significance
of what I was not seeing. The effect was dramatic.

When the final curtain fell I knew I had witnessed genius.
I jumped to my feet and applauded. 'Author!' I cried. 'Author!'
As the applause died down I climbed on stage, took a bow,
and with all due modesty, acknowledged the silence.

Say 'Ah!'

It hangs from the ceiling,
legs swinging. Zip
unfastening. My little grape.

Split uvula. Make a wish
and the palate is cleft.
Genetically a near miss.

A hair's breadth away
from a hare-lip
and thpeaking like thith.

Right as Rain

Alan's had his thingies done. You know, down there.
Hurt like hell at first but now he's fine.
He told us all about it in the bar.

The whole caboodle lasted half an hour.
Tied tightly with a sort of rubber twine
they drop off. Now Alan's right as rain. You know, down there.

Eighteen months ago he had a scare.
Blood in the pan was the ominous sign.
He told us all about it in the bar.

Unlike women, men don't really care
to talk about illness, it might undermine
the macho image. Especially when it's, you know, down there.

Making jokes about the bottom line
he gets them in, four lagers, two bitters and a dry white wine.
Alan's had his thingies done. You know, down there.
He told us all about it in the bar.

My Divine Juggler

Jugglers, as you can imagine,
are great fun to be with.
Mine is.
Alert and ambidextrous,
rarely dropping an aitch or missing a trick,
head in the air, clear-eyed and smiling,
I'm mad for him.

No couch potato he.
After a hard day in the busy town square
he comes home to prepare supper.
Under the spotlight in the kitchen
he works the vegetables, eight at a time.
Spins plates, tosses pans.
In orbit, knives hiss with pleasure.

In the bathroom, ducks and deodorants
spring to life in his hands.
Loofahs loop-the-loop. A Ferris Wheel
of shower-caps and shampoo bottles.
Flannels paraglide, soaps and sponges
dance a perfumed fandango.
I would die for him.

He will be the perfect father, I know it.
In the maternity ward he arrived,
laden with champagne and flowers.
Matron gasped, midwives giggled,
other mothers marvelled as the newlyborn
went spinning through the air like startled planets:
Mars, Mercury, Jupiter. Our triplets.
My divine juggler.

I Married A Human Cannonball

I married a human cannonball
Against my mother's wishes
One day he went ballistic
And started throwing dishes

So I left him for a fire-eater
Who, inflamed with wild desire,
Kissed me once so passionately
He set my hair on fire

Then an irresponsible hypnotist
Cast his irresistible spell
But my life as a chicken
Became a living hell

A clown moved in to make me laugh
Red nose and criss-cross eyes
But he never took his make-up off
And, oh, those custard pies

So I left him for a tightrope walker
But he became upset
When I wouldn't let him you-know-what
Without a safety net

But Fate at last, was kind to me
Now I'm as happy as a queen
For I live with the circus owner
And her name is Geraldine.

The Tallest Man in Britain

I was in a room with the tallest man in Britain
And of one thing I could be certain
In no other room in Britain was there a man taller.

He agreed when I pointed out how tall he was.
'And I bet people say that to you all the time.'
He smiled wearily. 'No, as a matter of fact you're the first.'

To get into the *Guinness Book of Records*
All he had to do was get out of bed one morning
And measure himself.

Easier than sitting in a bathtub with 35 rattlesnakes
Easier than holding 109 venomous bees in your mouth
Easier than balancing a motorbike on your teeth for 14.5 seconds
Easier than riding a lawnmower across the USA in 42 days
Easier than roller blading blindfold across the Sahara. Backwards.

'Wouldn't you rather be the *strongest* man in Britain?' I asked.
'Or the *fastest*? Or the *richest*?'
'No,' he said, 'I'm perfectly happy the way I am.'
And excusing himself, went off in search
Of somebody else to look down on.

The Perfect Crime

The sword-swallower
stabbed his unfaithful
wife to death

Before disposing
of the murder weapon
in one gulp.

Love Cycle

Up against the wall
Locked in passionate embrace
our two bicycles

M.I.L.T.

Blessed are the children and happy the spouses
Lucky the neighbours who every day meet
Mothers In Leather Trousers

Pushing their buggies in T-shirts or blouses
Swish-swash hear them shimmying down the street
Blessed are the children and happy the spouses

Bricklayer's labourers stop building houses
Scaffolders, road-diggers, drivers compete
To whistle at Mothers In Leather Trousers

South Kensington ladies, Brummies and Scousers
Sisterhood of bottoms large or petite
Blessed are the children and happy the spouses

What a smooth and beautiful skin the cows is
Especially when softened and buffed up a treat
By Mothers In Leather Trousers

What man hasn't turned and tripped over his feet?
Polished anthracite with the promise of heat
Blessed are the children and happy the spouses
Who live with Mothers In Leather Trousers.

No Message

At first, picture postcards
Next to my address:
A blank stare

The occasional letter
Envelope torn open to reveal:
An empty page

The late-night phone call
I recognize the intake of your breath
But no voice

Finally, the bottle
Washed up on the beach
by the morning tide

Pulling out the cork
I remove the slip of paper
In your handwriting it says:

'No Message.'

Sad Music

We fall to the earth like leaves
Lives as brief as footprints in snow
No words express the grief we feel
I feel I cannot let her go.

For she is everywhere.
Walking on the windswept beach
Talking in the sunlit square.
Next to me in the car
I see her sitting there.

At night she dreams me
and in the morning the sun does not rise.
My life is as thin as the wind
And I am done with counting stars.

She is gone, she is gone.
I am her sad music, and I play on, and on, and on.

The End

What I love about everyday
       is the touch wood at bumping into *one*
What I hate about *one*
       is bone, the finger pointing towards *death*
What I love about *death*
       is the No, No, No, No it joyfully *eclipses*
What I hate about *eclipses*
       is that one extinction may encourage *another*
What I love about *another*
       is the hoary chestnut shared in the face of *death*
What I hate about *death*
       is the lack of rehearsal time to perfect *one*
What I love about *one*
       is lone, it begins and ends open-mouthed at *birth*
What I hate about *birth*
       is the back-log of stars it invariably *eclipses*
What I love about *eclipses*
       is the sure-as-eggs that one leads to *another*
What I hate about *another*
       is the alter ego we might have been at *birth*
What I love about *birth*
       is the universal surprise, on the dot, *everyday*
What I hate about *everyday*
       is The End, the beginning of *eclipses*.

★　　★　　★

Acknowledgements

'Everyday Eclipses' was commissioned by the BBC World Service and subsequently appeared in the *Poetry Review*. 'Meeting the Poet at Victoria Station' was also published in *Poetry Review*. 'Pure Jaguar' was the result of a commission by Chester Zoo to celebrate the opening of the Jaguar Park. It was not submitted. 'In Two Minds,' is based on the poem 'A View of Things' by Edwin Morgan. 'No Message' was inspired by a cartoon by Douglas Maxwell. The line 'I am her sad music' is from 'Memorial' by Norman MacCaig, and the poem 'Sad Music' was written for Brian Boylan in memoriam Monique Beudert.

Answers to Riddles: (i) Tweezers (ii) The Plague